Schaum Generations

Wesley Schaum
Smart & Jazzy
Level 2

FOREWORD
This collection of fun-to-learn solos is based on popular music of various genres including ragtime, jazz, blues and boogie. The contemporary sounds and syncopated rhythms provide fascinating educational material as well as valuable technical studies.

INDEX
At the Max	2
Big Beat	7
Bouncin' Beetle	16
Bugle Woogle	12
Cool School	4
Easy Come, Easy Go	8
Empty Pocket Blues	11
Rockin' Rhythm	6
Go Man Go!	10
Solid Stomp	14
Swingin' Tiger	13
Take It Easy	3

Schaum Publications, Inc. • 10235 N. Port Washington Rd. • Mequon, WI 53092
www.schaumpiano.net

© Copyright 2013, 1971 and 1966 by Schaum Publications, Inc., Mequon, Wisconsin
International Copyright Secured • All Rights Reserved • Printed in U.S.A.
ISBN-13: 978-1-62906-000-2

Warning: The reproduction of any part of this publication without prior written consent of Schaum Publications, Inc. is prohibited by U.S. Copyright Law and subject to penalty. This prohibition includes all forms of printed media (including any method of photocopy), all forms of electronic media (including computer images), all forms of film media (including filmstrips, transparencies, slides and movies), all forms of sound recordings (including cassette tapes and compact disks), and all forms of video media (including video tapes and DVD).

At the Max

Take It Easy

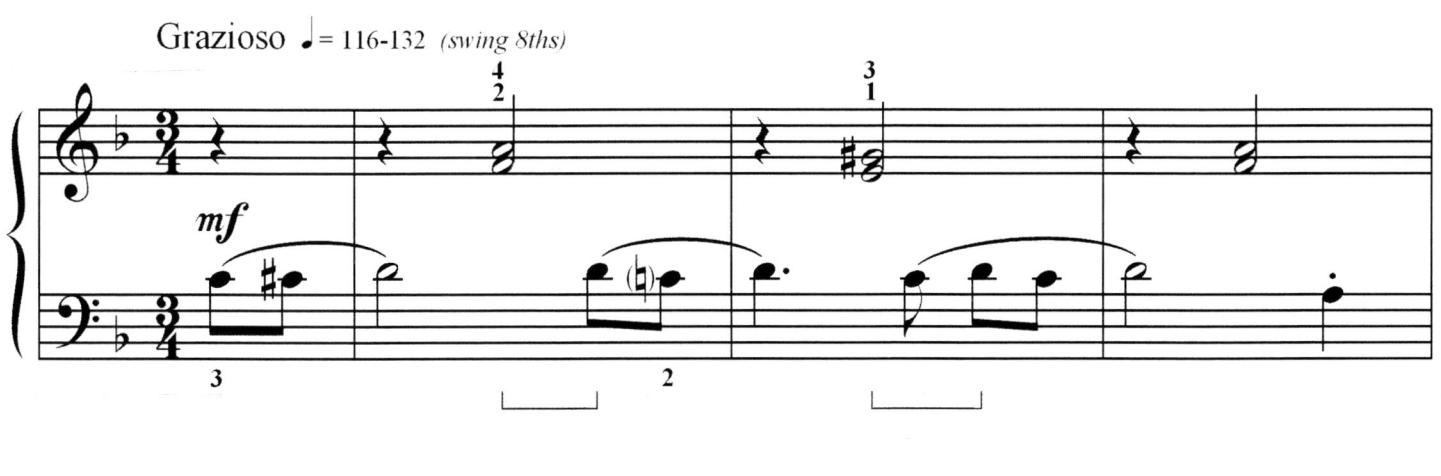
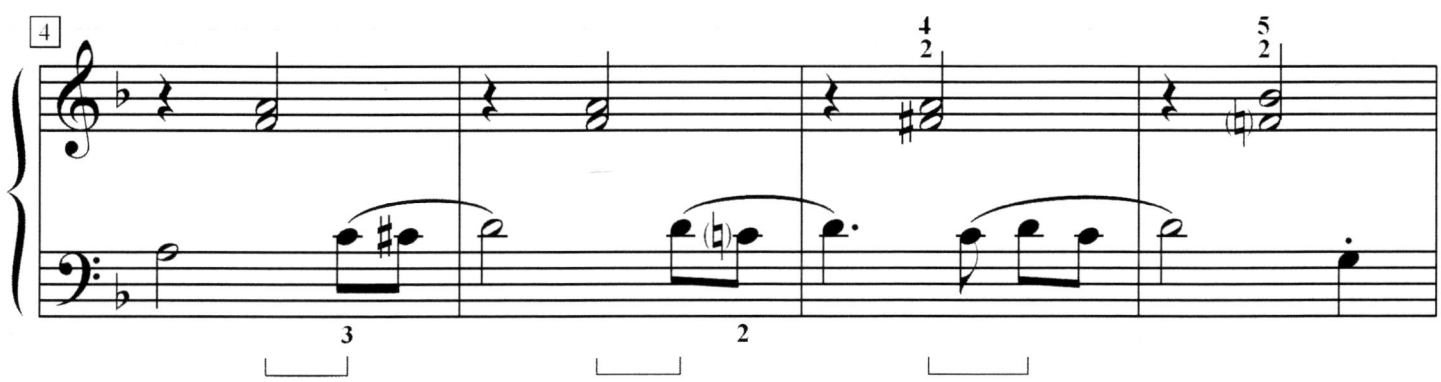

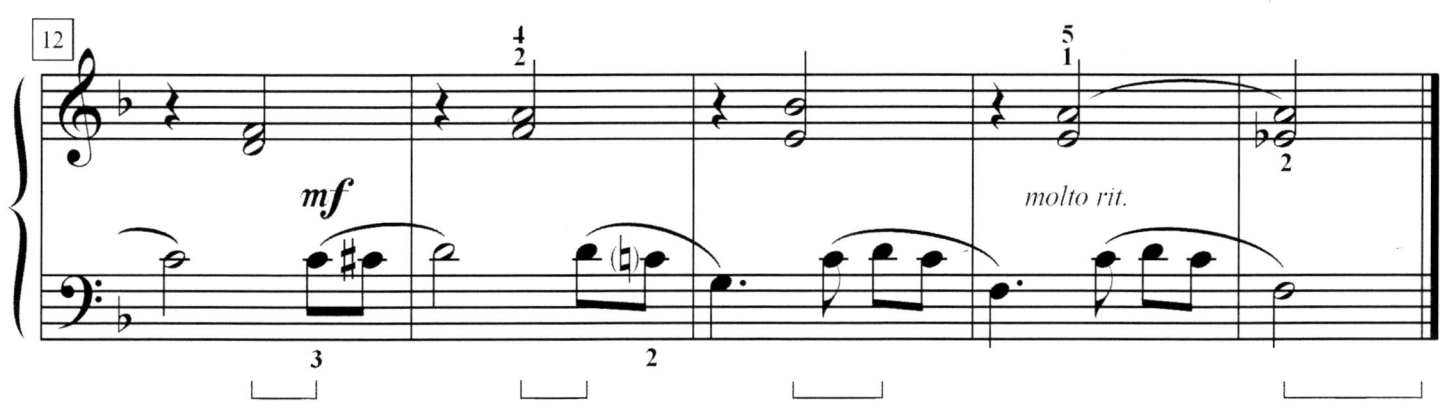

Cool School

Rockin' Rhythm

Big Beat

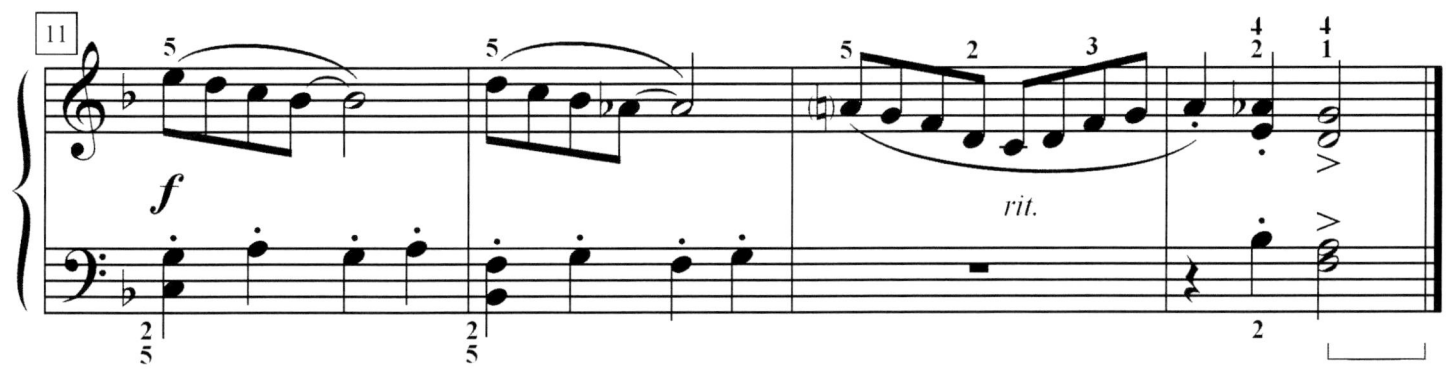

Easy Come, Easy Go

Go Man Go!

Empty Pocket Blues

Moderato ♩= 96-104 *(swing 8ths)*

Play L.H. one octave lower throughout.

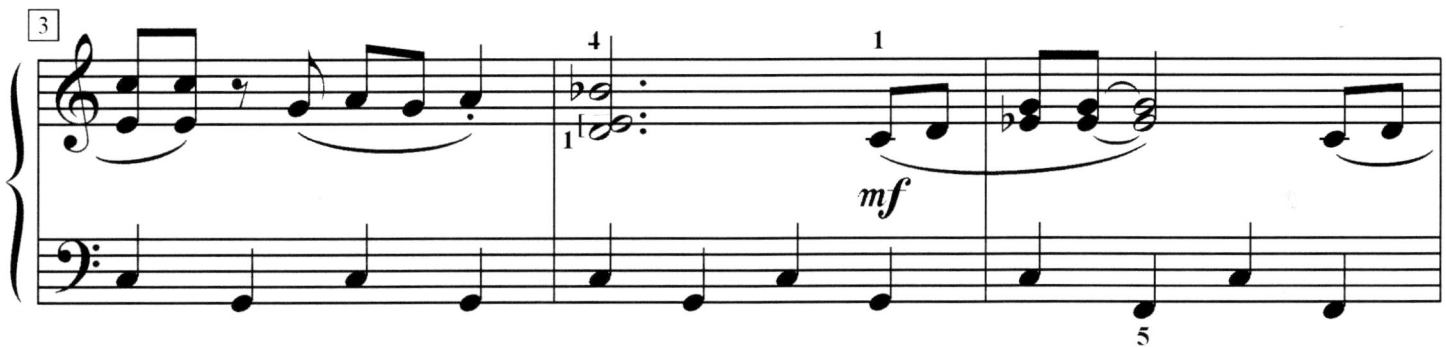

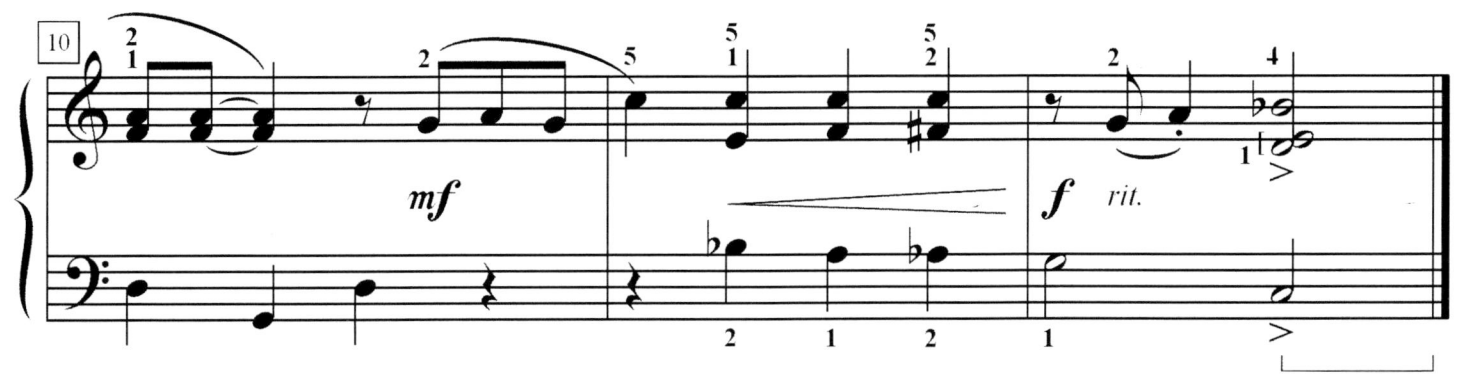

Bugle Woogle

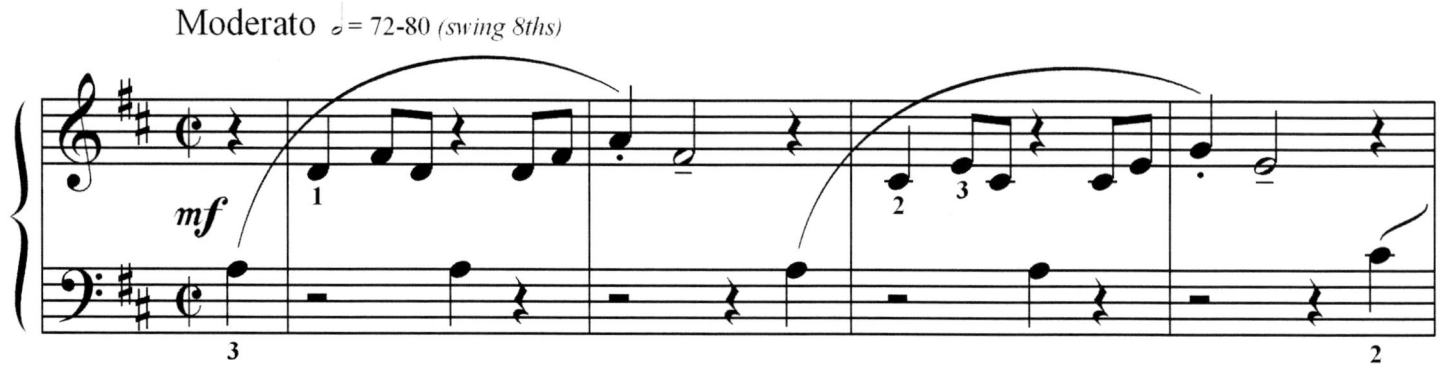

Swingin' Tiger

Solid Stomp

Bouncin' Beetle